ARCHITECTURE TOURS L.A. GUIDEBOOK
W. HOLLYWOOD-BEVERLY HILLS

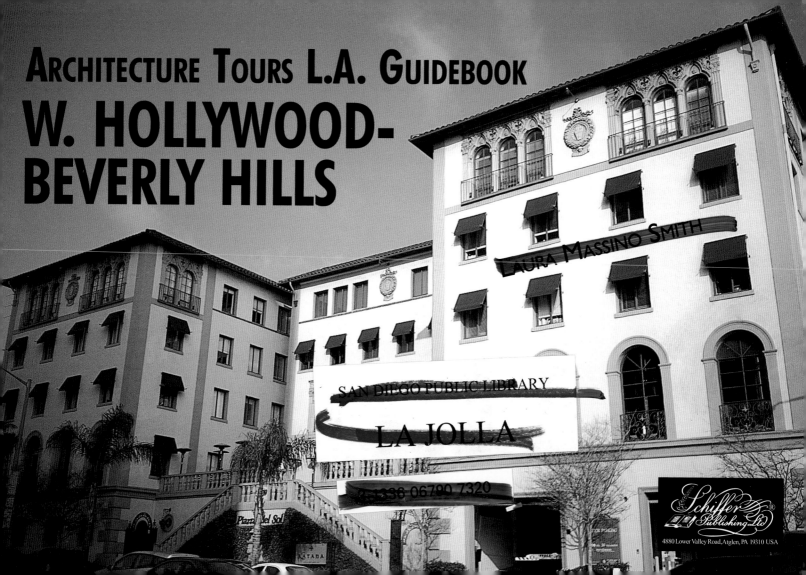

Architecture Tours L.A. Guidebook
W. Hollywood-
Beverly Hills

Laura Massino Smith

Schiffer Publishing Ltd

4880 Lower Valley Road, Atglen, PA 19310 USA

Library of Congress Cataloging-in-Publication Data

Smith, Laura Massino.
    Architecture tours L.A. guidebook : W. Hollywood-Beverly Hills / by Laura Massino Smith.
        p. cm.
    ISBN 0-7643-2122-6 (pbk.)
1. Architecture—California—West Hollywood—Tours. 2. Architecture—California—Beverly Hills—Tours. 3. Automobile travel—California—West Hollywood—Tours. 4. Automobile travel—California—Beverly Hills—Tours. 5. West Hollywood (Calif.)—Buildings, structures, etc.—Tours. 6. Beverly Hills (Calif.)—Buildings, structures, etc.—Tours. I. Title: W. Hollywood-Beverly Hills. II. Title.
    NA735.W465S64 2004
    720'.9794'94—dc22
                                    2004014289

Designed by John P. Cheek
Type set in Futura BdCn BT/Humanist 521 LT BT

ISBN: 0-7643-2122-6
Printed in China
1 2 3 4

DEDICATION
To my extraordinary husband, Drew, whose undying love, patience, encouragement, and support have guided me to discover my true passion.

Published by Schiffer Publishing Ltd.
4880 Lower Valley Road
Atglen, PA 19310
Phone: (610) 593-1777; Fax: (610) 593-2002
E-mail: Info@schifferbooks.com

For the largest selection of fine reference books on this and related subjects, please visit our web site at www.schifferbooks.com
We are always looking for people to write books on new and related subjects. If you have an idea for a book please contact us at the above address.

This book may be purchased from the publisher.
Include $3.95 for shipping.
Please try your bookstore first.
You may write for a free catalog.

In Europe, Schiffer books are distributed by
Bushwood Books
6 Marksbury Ave.
Kew Gardens
Surrey TW9 4JF England
Phone: 44 (0) 20 8392-8585; Fax: 44 (0) 20 8392-9876
E-mail: info@bushwoodbooks.co.uk
Free postage in the U.K., Europe; air mail at cost.

ARCHITECTURE TOURS L.A.

www.architecturetoursla.com
323.464.7868

Architecture Tours L.A. specializes in guided driving tours led by an architectural historian in a 1962 vintage Cadillac. Our tours focus on the historic and significant contemporary architecture in Los Angeles, highlighting the cultural aspects of the history of the city's built environment. This guidebook will allow you to drive yourself and discover L.A. in your own car, at your own pace. In addition to WEST HOLLYWOOD/BEVERLY HILLS, other tours offered by Architecture Tours L.A. include:

HOLLYWOOD
HANCOCK PARK/MIRACLE MILE
DOWNTOWN
SILVER LAKE
PASADENA
FRANK GEHRY

Disclaimer

It is not advisable for anyone operating a motor vehicle to read this book. Please pull your car into a safe, designated parking area before attempting any fine print. Better yet, take this tour with a friend who can act as navigator and narrator. Naturally, the best way to see it all is riding shotgun with the author!

Neither the author nor the publisher assumes responsibility for moving violations committed while intoxicated by this tour.

Note to Tour Goers

The sites included in this self-guided tour represent the architectural highlights of the WEST HOLLYWOOD/BEVERLY HILLS area. This tour is meant to be an overview, a starting point of sorts, and is intended to give the participant a feeling for the neighborhood. By no means does the tour include everything of interest. Numerous books of ponderous proportions have been written to that end, and if your interest is piqued, you might refer to the bibliography in the back of this book for further reading.

Herein, within a matter of hours you will glean a pretty good understanding of what historically happened, and what is currently happening architecturally in WEST HOLLYWOOD/BEVERLY HILLS. The photographs herein are for quick identification of what you will be seeing up close, in full scale.

The criteria for inclusion into this guidebook consist of the historical, cultural, and architectural significance of each site, and the fact that it can be seen relatively easily from the street. So relax and have a great ride!

INTRODUCTION

West Hollywood and Beverly Hills are independent cities separate from the city of Los Angeles; each with its own city hall, police force, and government. West Hollywood was originally called "Sherman," after Moses Sherman who had his railroad and rail yard here, and was incorporated in 1984. Beverly Hills, known worldwide as the home of celebrities and movie stars, was named after a town called Beverly Farm in Massachusetts and incorporated in 1914. Both cities had their beginnings as Mexican ranchos where agriculture was the main industry. Cattle ranches occupied West Hollywood, while lima bean fields dominated the Beverly Hills landscape. Commercial and residential development started after the railroads connecting the Midwest and East Coast to California came through in the late 1870s, but much of the development occurred in the 1920s and after. The architectural styles popular in the 1920s were Art Deco, Spanish Colonial Revival, Spanish Mediterranean, and other European-derived revival styles such as English Tudor and French Provincial. "Storybook" architecture, a kind of "Hansel and Gretel" influenced style, and Islamic-inspired architectural styles were also popular during this time period. One of the best examples of Art Deco architecture in all of Los Angeles is found in West Hollywood on the Sunset Strip in what is now the Argyle Hotel. One of the most well known examples of "Storybook" architecture is found in Beverly Hills in the Witch's House, a whimsical home that looks as though it might have once belonged to a witch. The Late Art Deco style known as Streamline Moderne is also found here in a duplex in West Hollywood, and one of the few (if only) examples of the Art Nouveau style in southern California can be seen in Beverly Hills.

Frank Lloyd Wright built structures in both cities, as did his son. Buildings by other influential architects including Rudolf M. Schindler, whose own home was built in 1922, Craig Ellwood's 1960 Mid-Century Modern office building, and Frank Gehry's 1979 Gemini Galley are all located in West Hollywood.

I.M. Pei's CAA office building, The Museum of Television and Radio – Richard Meier's "other" museum – is in Beverly Hills, as are offices and restaurants in the Post-modern style by Morphosis and Richard Keating of Skidmore Owings and Merrill.

In West Hollywood, smaller scale residences and high density commercial areas like the Sunset Strip on Sunset Blvd. and Santa Monica Blvd. were major areas of activity and have been through many changes. In the 1940s the Sunset Strip was lined with elegant nightclubs, like Ciro's, where people wore tuxedos and evening gowns. In the 1960s the hippie generation took over with rock clubs, where denim jeans and flower power were en vogue. A railroad once ran in the center median along Santa Monica Blvd., once a dirty, industrial area, which now enjoys an active retail, restaurant, and nightclub scene.

In Beverly Hills, the Beverly Hills Hotel acted as a beacon to attract people west from Downtown in the early days. The Spanish Mission style hotel was built in 1912 as one of the first hotels in the area, and now is one of the most elegant and refined establishments, hosting celebrities of all sorts. The "flats" of Beverly Hills, an area once referred to as just "Beverly" (the hills were called "Beverly Hills"), have slightly curved streets with specific trees planted on specific streets and the architectural styles are mostly European-derived revival styles. When Mary Pickford and Douglas Fairbanks built their home, "Pickfair," in 1920, other people in the movie industry followed them and thus initiated Beverly Hills' status as "home of the stars." Beverly Hills is also home to late 20th century architectural styles including Post-modern. Buildings with their structural steel I-beams intentionally left exposed are a response to the pristine glass and steel (or wood) Mid-Century Modern box. The Deconstructivist buildings use industrial materials in a way that elevates them to a level of beauty as seen in office buildings and restaurants on Wilshire Boulevard.

As you drive through you will see the history of these very different cities expressed in the wildly varying styles of architecture that coexist very harmoniously.

On Beverly Blvd. between La Cienega Blvd. and San Vicente Blvd.

1) This site was originally occupied by a children's amusement park with rides for younger children before the Beverly Center shopping mall was built. The most remarkable part of the mall's exterior are the outside escalators. They bear a striking resemblance to those of the Pompidou Centre in Paris, where the workings of the building are on the exterior. They can be seen here with glass ceilings and red neon stripes.

1) Beverly Center, 1982, Welton Becket and Associates, 8500 BEVERLY BOULEVARD

From Beverly Blvd.
Turn right on La Cienega Blvd.
Turn right on San Vicente
Bear left, this becomes Burton Way

You are now driving on Burton Way, which was named after Burton Green, who was from Massachusetts and named Beverly Hills after his hometown, Beverly Farm. He was also a very important figure in the planning of Beverly Hills as a "Garden City." You will notice lush landscaping throughout the city. The city was called "Beverly" at first and only the area north of Sunset Blvd. was called "Beverly Hills." Now it is all known as Beverly Hills and has come a very long way from its very humble beginnings. Rancho Rodeo de Las Aguas was the original name of this area. "Ranch of the Gathering of the Waters" was owned by Juan Batista Valdez, and his 4,500-acre ranch was eventually sold in 1854 for $4,000. Charles Denker and Henry Hammel bought the land and planted a lima bean field. In 1900 The Amalgamated Oil Company bought the property and started drilling for oil. Oil rigs are still pumping at Beverly Hills High School and at the Beverly Center, now cleverly hidden. In 1907 parcels of land began to be sold for residential development and in 1914 Beverly Hills was incorporated with a population of 550 people. It remains to this day a separate city from Los Angeles, with its own city hall and police force. In 1920 Douglas Fairbanks and Mary Pickford built their home, "Pickfair," in Beverly Hills, after which other celebrities followed them to the area. Thus setting the stage for Beverly Hills' claim to fame as the home of the stars.

2) Beverly Hills Municipal Court, 1968, Maurice Fleishman, 9355 BURTON WAY

2) Here on your right, just past Foothill Road, the building with the large white columns in front is a fairly typical 1960s design for a civic structure. It is clad in dark grey granite panels and uses a type of split brick on its surface. This courthouse has seen many celebrity cases including those of Winona Ryder and Courtney Love.

3) Here on your right, at the intersection of Rexford Drive and Burton Way, is the back of Beverly Hills City Hall. What is most visible here is the expansion designed by Charles Moore in 1992 to house the library, police, and additional offices. The original City Hall was designed by William Gage in the Spanish Colonial Revival style. An attractive tower with a colorful mosaic tile dome marks the 1932 structure, which you will see later from the front.

3) **Beverly Hills City Hall, 1932, William J. Gage, Expansion, 1992, Charles Moore, 450 North Crescent Drive**

4) The addition to the Civic Center was created with a sensitivity towards the older structure and a desire to create a new structure that would blend harmoniously with the old. Colorful tiles, which reference the mosaic dome, are used in the new building. You will see the front later.

4) Beverly Hills Civic Center, 1992, Charles Moore (Urban Innovations Group), 444 NORTH REXFORD DRIVE

5) Here on your left is the stark, white, Georgian Revival style office building that African-American architect Paul Williams designed for MCA, which was part of Universal at the time. His concept was to design an inviting building by making it look like a grand family home complete with green wood shutters and front door with a triangular neo-Classical pediment above. The white brick and stately columns create the serious, yet gracious, atmosphere Williams was so well known for. The design is very similar to residential designs by Williams.

5) Music Corporation of America (MCA), Litton Industries (now Global Crossing Plaza), 1940, Paul Williams, 360 NORTH CRESCENT DRIVE

 **Turn right on Wilshire Blvd.**

10) On your right, at the northeast corner of the intersection, is the Indian Fountain, which was built with funds donated by the Beverly Hills residents living north of Santa Monica Blvd. in honor of the original inhabitants of the area, the Tongva, or Gabrielino Indians.

10) Indian Fountain, 1931, Ralph Flewelling, Merrell Gage, CORNER OF SANTA MONICA BLVD. AND WILSHIRE BLVD.

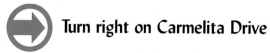 **Turn right on Carmelita Drive**

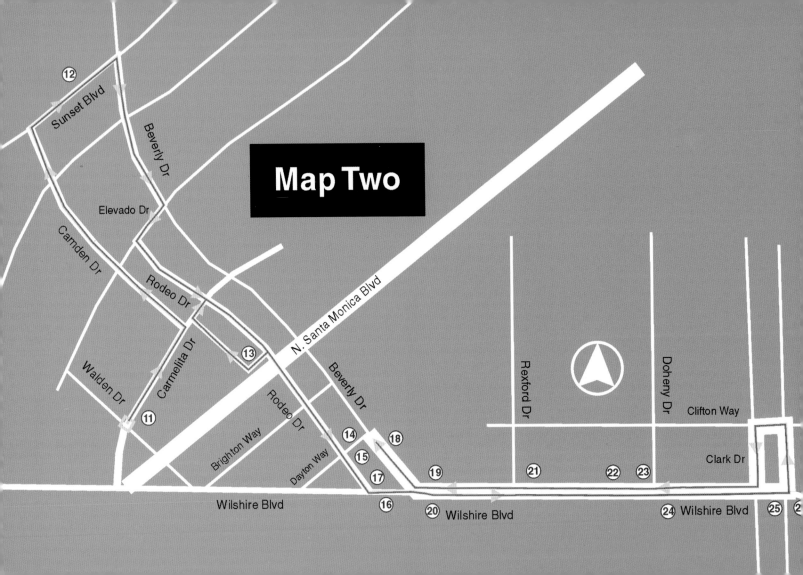

Map Two

11) This distinctive house on the right was moved to this site in 1934. Originally designed by an art director/set designer for the Willat Studio in Culver City, it was moved here when the studio closed. It was used in a number of films and also as production offices, and is affectionately known as "The Witch's House." Notice the steeply sloped, curving roof with irregularly shaped shingles, odd windows, and moat complete with bridge. This is the style of architecture now known as "Storybook," which was popular in the 1920s and 1930s.

11) Spadena House, 1921, Henry (Harry) Oliver, 516 NORTH WALDEN DRIVE

Turn left on Camden Drive

Spanish Mediterranean, English Tudor and French Provincial Revival architectural styles are dominant in Beverly Hills. Neo-Classical-inspired mansions and Craftsman houses are seen here, too, along with flat-roofed Mid-Century Modern homes and everything in between. The European-derived styles are the most popular, though, and you will notice many French Mansard-type roofs used liberally and "mini-Versailles"-type mansions. It is an eclectic array that expresses the homeowners' individual preferences.

Notice the curve of the road and also notice that only one type of tree is planted along each street. On Camden Drive are magnolia trees. On other streets you will see all ficus trees or all palm trees. Part of the plan for a "Garden City" – developed by Wilbur Cook, who had worked with Central Park's designer Frederick Law Olmstead, and horticulturist John J. Reeves, who developed the plan for the trees – this was done to maintain uniformity of each street's appearance. The curve of the street adds to the visual effect, so that when looking north, all that one sees are trees. This is also a good way to slow down traffic, make the ride more meandering, and break up the rigidity of the grid system.

Turn right on Sunset Blvd.

12) Here on your left, across Sunset Blvd., is the famous Beverly Hills Hotel, which was built in 1912, two years before Beverly Hills was incorporated. It was built to attract people to come west from Downtown. The earliest residents of Los Angeles all lived in and around the Downtown area, and in the first years of the 20th century, it took quite some time to get to Beverly Hills. In the early days, the hotel was used as a community center and also had a movie theater before any other theaters were built in Beverly Hills. Designed in the Spanish Mission style with a central arch flanked by two green domes, the hotel was expanded and remodeled from 1947-1951, and again with more additions and alterations in 1959 by architect Paul Williams, whose MCA building was seen earlier. The structure was expanded on its eastern side with the tall wall with the name of the hotel written in elegant white letters and the green-and-white striped awning. The hotel sits on more than twelve lushly landscaped acres and has more than two hundred rooms and twenty-one private bungalows. It was renovated and updated in 1995 by the owner, the Sultan of Brunei, for $200 million, but it retains much of the original design. Of course, this hotel is known for its famous guests including Cecil B. DeMille, Mary Pickford, and Douglas Fairbanks, who would have drinks in the Polo Lounge, as well as the Rat Pack's Frank Sinatra and Dean Martin. Tony Bennett and George Hamilton have also been spotted here and Elizabeth Taylor spent some of her honeymoons here.

12) Beverly Hills Hotel, 1912, Elmer Grey, Re-model, 1947-51 and 1959, Paul Williams, 9641 Sunset Blvd.

 Turn right on Beverly Drive

Notice the alternating varieties of palm trees on this street

**Right on Elevado Drive
Left on Rodeo Drive
Pass Carmelita Drive and just a
little north of Santa Monica Blvd.**

13) Here on your right is one of most unique houses in the city. Painted white and blue and with an arched, carved wood front door, it was built in the Art Nouveau style, popular in France, Belgium, and Spain in the late 1800s and into the early 1900s, but not so in the United States. This style of architecture is rarely seen anywhere in this country, which makes it a very unique house, indeed. Although it was built in the late 20th century, it is reminiscent of the work of Spanish architect Antonio Gaudi. Hardly a ninety-degree angle is to be found here; instead, free-flowing and curvilinear forms compose this house. Sinuous relief sculpture decorates the exterior and the curves and sculpture continue on the inside, as well as on the back of the house. On the back, the sculpture depicts two opposing peacocks with the image of a woman in the middle. The metal grillwork also has been made in the image of a peacock. Notice the girls dancing around the chimney. The backyard is more like an interior yard enclosed by walls, as most of these properties are. Alleys in back provide a service entrance for garbage pick-up and other practical necessities. This house was designed in this style for a collection of Art Nouveau furniture.

13) O'Neill House, 1984, Santa Monica Architectural Group (Tom Oswald, Don Ramos), 507 NORTH RODEO DRIVE

**Turn right into the alley
Go around to the back of
the house
Turn right out of the alley
onto Carmelita Avenue
Right on Rodeo Drive
Stay in the left lane
Pass Brighton Way**

14) Look to your left, passing the Armani, Ralph Lauren, and Bernini Brothers shops. Just past the Bally shop and inset from the street, you will see walls of glass and white with a tall, angular central white spire. This is a structure that was designed by Frank Lloyd Wright towards the end of his career. It is one of the few storefronts that isn't flat. This was built as a mini-mall, of sorts, for a former showgirl, then wealthy widow, named Nina Anderton, who wanted all of her favorite designer shops in one place. Using the same concept for circulation as he did in the Guggenheim Museum in New York, Wright creates a spiral, yet angular ramp that takes you up to the top of the three stories and back down again. Large expanses of glass allow the passerby to look at what's for sale.

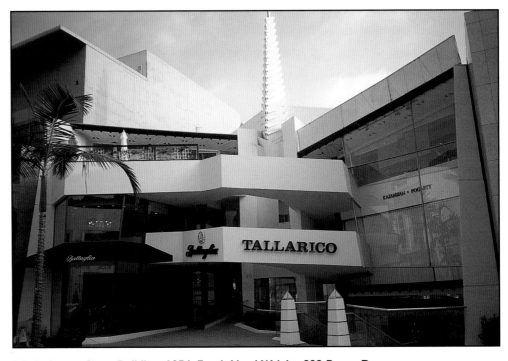

14) Anderton Court Building, 1954, Frank Lloyd Wright, 332 Rodeo Drive

15) Further down the street on your left, at the corner of Rodeo Drive and Dayton Way, is another shopping center. A cobblestone street winds upwards to the top, passing exclusive shops such as Iceberg, Gianfranco Ferre, and Versace on the way. This was designed as a pastiche to a European town, with its narrow street, replicas of Neo-Classical architecture, and Old World feel. Here you will find upscale shops and restaurants, and a concierge in a long red coat and top hat standing on the corner giving people directions and other advice.

16) Directly in front of you, at the end of the commercial part of Rodeo Drive, is the Regent Beverly Wilshire Hotel, built by the architects who designed many structures in Los Angeles, including the Oviatt Building, the Fine Arts Building in Downtown L.A., and the Taft Building in Hollywood. This hotel was designed in the Italian Renaissance Revival style based in 14th-17th century Europe. Characteristics of this style include a flat roof with a crowning cornice supported by modillion brackets, often with dentil ornamentation and arched windows. The first floor displays Neo-Classical columns and Spanish Colonial Revival decorative ornamentation in the form of shield shapes, medallions, and floral forms. Here since the 1920s, the hotel's claim to fame is that it was used in the movie *Pretty Woman* as the location for the transformation of a young woman. This building is listed on the National Register of Historic Places.

15) Two Rodeo Drive, 1990, Kaplin, McLaughlin and Diaz, 2 RODEO DRIVE

16) Regent Beverly Wilshire Hotel, 1926, Walker & Eisen, 9500 WILSHIRE BLVD.

Turn left on Wilshire Blvd.

17) Here on your left, at the corner of Wilshire Blvd. and Beverly Drive, is the elegantly curving Bank of America Building. All of the corners are rounded, and the front of the building addresses the intersection with its concave shape and superimposed granite grid. The windows are recessed to provide shade from the sun, and the structure is clad in small, elegant white marble tiles.

17) Bank of America Building, 1960, Victor Gruen Associates, 9461 WILSHIRE BLVD.

18) Across the street on Beverly Drive are the remains of what was once a wonderful movie palace. Fashioned after the Taj Mahal in India with a large central onion dome, an arched façade in front and palm trees once completed the illusion. It is currently threatened with demolition. The structure in front was built much later, hiding the theater behind.

18) The Beverly Theater, 1925, L.A. Smith, 202 BEVERLY DRIVE

19) California National Bank (now Sterling Plaza), 1929, John and Donald Parkinson, 9441 Wilshire Blvd.

19) On your left, on the northeast corner of the intersection, is the magnificent white and gold Art Deco bank building. It was designed by the same architects who designed Union Station and other buildings Downtown, and Bullock's Wilshire Department Store further east on Wilshire Blvd. Full of angular shapes and geometric surface decoration in gold, it embodies all of the characteristics of Art Deco architecture.

20) Here on your right, across the street, is a fairly recent building of the late 20th century. Angled concrete vertical elements stress its height and make you want to look to the top, which when you do, reveal a wonderful, stained glass flat top, which is very playful and unexpected.

20) Re-Max Building, c. 1970, Langdon & Wilson, 9454 Wilshire Blvd.

21) Here on your left, at the corner of Rexford Drive and Wilshire Blvd., was originally a Home Savings and Loan (owned by the Ahmanson family), which were all designed by Millard Sheets in the 1950s and 1960s. All are of box form, usually clad in travertine tile and with inlaid mosaics. You can still see the inlaid vertical bands with the letters "H S & L" for Home Savings and Loan remaining. The mosaic has a painterly quality because Sheets was also a prolific painter whose paintings are still quite desirable now. Look for his signature in the lower left corner of the central mosaic.

22) First Bank, c. 1959, Millard Sheets and S. David Underwood, 9145 Wilshire Blvd.

21) Home Savings and Loan (now Washington Mutual), 1955, Millard Sheets, 9245 Wilshire Blvd.

22) Further down the street on your left is another bank building, also owned by the Ahmanson family and designed by Millard Sheets. You can see the mosaics here, too, on the front. On the side, this building also has a beautiful white molded shade structure decorated with birds and flowers.

23) Next, on your left at the corner of Wilshire Blvd. and Doheny Drive, is a restaurant called Kate Mantilini. Mantilini was a 1930s boxing promoter and ballerina. She was also the restaurant owner's uncle's mistress, and quite a spunky lady! On the interior you can find a mural of boxers Marvin Hagler and Thomas Hearns from the famous Hagler/Hearns fight of the mid-1980s in honor of Kate. This restaurant was designed by Morphosis, with principal architects Thom Mayne and Michael Rotondi at the time. It is reflective of the Post-modern style of architecture, which began in the 1960s and still continues today. The concept is that of exploration and expression. Exploration of usage of industrial materials in unusual ways, and expression of structure and technology. It is meant for you to see the "bones" of the structure, revealing exposed I-beams and allowing the structure to be expressed on the outside of the building. Horizontal beams extend beyond the outer walls and are capped with four black tiles. More down the street...

24) Coming up on your right is another example of Post-modern architecture. Here, the corner walls of the outside of the building are missing and the green patinated structural I-beams are completely exposed. The wall in front also appears incomplete. This concept has to do with the notion of exposed construction and urban decay. You are shown the composition of the structure by making it look as though the walls have been removed. This building houses offices of another one of the top talent agencies in Los Angeles.

24) ICM (International Creative Management), 1990, Richard Keating, (Skidmore, Owings & Merrill), 8942 WILSHIRE BLVD.

23) Kate Mantilini Restaurant, 1987, Morphosis, 8750 WILSHIRE BLVD.

25) Further down on your right, at the southwest corner of Wilshire Blvd. and Robertson Blvd., is a building from the 1920s designed in the Art Deco style. Stylized floral forms and angular shapes characterize the Art Deco style of the 1920s. The name Art Deco came from an exhibition in Paris in the early 1920s, with a name that translates to "Exhibition of Industrial and Decorative Arts," hence the name Art Deco.

25) Art Deco Building, c. 1929, The Austin Company of California, 8810 WILSHIRE **B**LVD.
(8800 WILSHIRE **B**LVD.**)**

26) On the southeast corner is one of the few buildings in Los Angeles designed by Arquitectonica, the firm based in Florida. A green steel grid system of sorts is used here for the window fenestration. The lower corner of the structure looks as though it has been removed, and serves to define the building's entrance. On the Wilshire Blvd. side of the building a concave black granite and glass wall was created to contrast the other rigid side of the building. Offices here are for the bank, BMG is the European music organization, and also Windham Hill music group and Tower Imaging, where X-rays and similar medical exams are conducted.

 Turn left on Robertson Blvd.
Left on Clifton Way
Left on Clark Drive
Right on Wilshire Blvd.

26) Wilshire-Robertson Plaza (Bank of America and BMG), 1990, Arquitectonica, 8760 Wilshire Blvd. (8750 Wilshire Blvd.)

Now as you head back on Wilshire Blvd., you will have a chance to take another look at what you saw minutes ago...

 Turn right on Beverly Drive

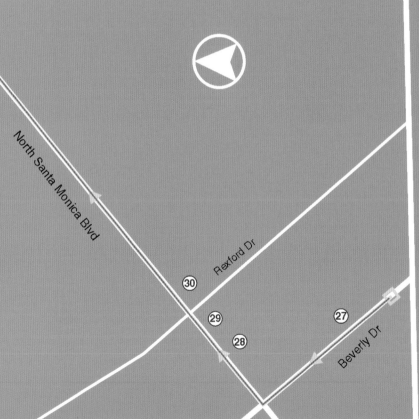

Map Three

Vista Grande St

N. Doheny Dr

North Santa Monica Blvd

Rexford Dr

30

29

28

27

Beverly Dr

27) On the right side of the street, past Dayton Way, is a small, unassuming black storefront, which is the Taschen bookstore. The glass entrance is framed in a large, black picture frame. The bookstore was recently designed by French architect Philippe Starck, and is a sumptuous, elegant, breathtaking space that must be experienced from the inside. The richness of materials along with the display of books and art create a visually delightful space.

27) Taschen Bookstore, 2003, Philippe Starck, 354 North Beverly Drive

Another opportunity to see some of what you saw earlier: On your left, at the corner of Beverly Drive and South Santa Monica Blvd., is the Museum of Television and Radio at 465 North Beverly Drive. More noticeable from this direction is the large circular glass form where the main entrance is.

Right on North Santa Monica Blvd.

28) On your right is the Beverly Hills Post Office built in the early 1930s in the Italian Renaissance style. Built of Roman brick, with both triangular and curved pediments above the door and windows, there are also quoins articulating the corners and a crowning cornice with modillion bracketing. Vacant since 1993, and now owned by the Beverly Hills Cultural Foundation, there are currently plans to convert it to a performance space with hopes that local celebrity residents will perform in plays there. This building is listed on the National Register of Historic Places.

28) Beverly Hills Post Office, 1933, Ralph Flewelling; Allison & Allison (consulting architects), 470 NORTH CANON DRIVE (469 NORTH CRESCENT DRIVE)

29) Now on your right is the front of Beverly Hills City Hall. The tower with its gleaming mosaic dome shows the Moorish influence of Spanish Colonial Revival architecture.

29) Beverly Hills City Hall, 1932, William J. Gage, 450 NORTH CRESCENT DRIVE

30) Directly next to the City Hall is the expansion of the Civic Center, which now houses the police department, the library, and other civic offices, seen earlier from the back. It was very sensitively designed by Charles Moore, incorporating the mosaic tile motif from the dome in the vertical engaged pilasters. Through the wide arch, an arched colonnade exaggerates the forms and is very playful, yet gives the serious air a civic center should have. This is an example of Historic Eclectic Post-modern architecture where historical forms are referenced and then re-interpreted.

30) Beverly Hills Civic Center, 1992, Charles Moore (Urban Innovations Group), 444 NORTH REXFORD DRIVE

Now on the border of West Hollywood and Beverly Hills at Santa Monica Blvd. and Doheny Drive, notice the wide center median. It was much wider at one point, when the trains ran down the middle of it.

West Hollywood was originally called "Sherman," after Moses Sherman who built his Los Angeles Railway here. The railway yards were on 5 1/2 acres surrounding Santa Monica Blvd. and San Vicente Blvd. and were located on the present site of the Pacific Design Center (seen later). Moses Sherman is the same Sherman of Sherman Oaks and Sherman Way in the San Fernando Valley, which he developed. Sherman's enterprise eventually partnered with Henry Huntington's Red Car trolleys that ran throughout Los Angeles County. The trains went all the way to the beach and all the way Downtown through an extensive system, but were dismantled due to increased auto traffic. The last trolley stopped running in 1941 and the last cargo train ran down Santa Monica Blvd. in 1965.

As early as the 1920s, the name of the area was changed to West Hollywood so as to have that association with Hollywood, which was a glamorous place then. The boundaries of West Hollywood run east to west from Doheny Drive to La Brea Avenue, and run north to south from Beverly Blvd. to Sunset Blvd., an area of about two square miles. There are approximately 37,000 residents who come from all walks of life; however, there is a large gay population and a large Russian immigrant population living here.

At its earliest, West Hollywood was comprised of Mexican ranchos, but when the population started coming from the Mid-West and the East Coast, the ranchos were eventually sold off for residential and commercial development. The area was home at one time or another to celebrities including Marilyn Monroe, Shelly Winters, Frank Sinatra, and silent screen cowboy actor William S. Hart, among others. In 1984, West Hollywood was incorporated and like Beverly Hills, also has its own police force, city hall, and mayor, separate from Los Angeles. It is also called "The Creative City," due to the large concentration of design and design-related businesses and music and music-related businesses.

**Turn left on Doheny Drive
Right on Vista Grande Street**

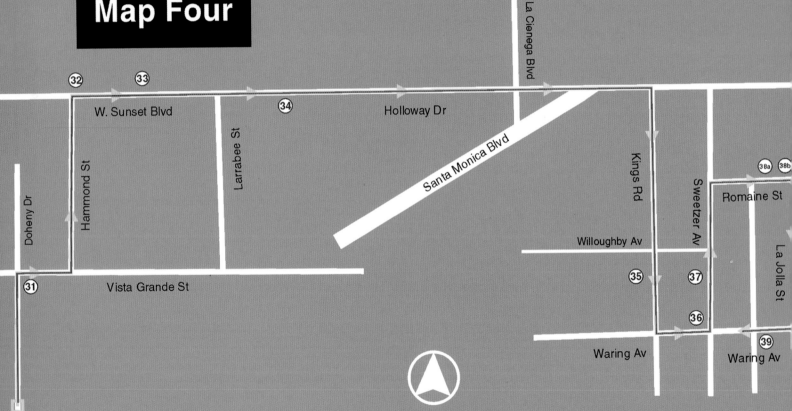

Map Four

③② ③③
W. Sunset Blvd
③④ Holloway Dr
La Cienega Blvd
Hammond St
Larrabee St
Doheny Dr
Santa Monica Blvd
Kings Rd
Sweetzer Av
③⑧ᵃ ③⑧ᵇ
Romaine St
Willoughby Av
La Jolla St
③① Vista Grande St
③⑤ ③⑦
③⑥
Waring Av ③⑨
Waring Av

31) Here on the corner is the home of Lloyd Wright. The house is a series of concrete boxes decorated with molded "textile block"-type bricks, similar to what his father used in four houses he designed here (one seen later). Notice the abstract form of the bricks, which use a tree motif as inspiration. High clerestory windows let light into the space. This house is listed on the National Register of Historic Places.

Born in 1890, Frank Lloyd Wright, Jr. was the oldest of Wright's six children and also an architect. He worked in Boston at the offices of Frederick Law Olmstead, the landscape designer of Central Park and many other urban parks. He studied landscaping and the relationship between houses and their landscaped environments. He came to Los Angeles in 1913 and worked on many of his father's projects including the Hollyhock House (seen on the HOLLYWOOD tour). Los Angeles, being the center of the movie industry, gave him an opportunity to work briefly at Paramount Studios as a designer. He designed many houses in Los Angeles, but his best know structure is the Wayfarer's Chapel in Palos Verdes, south of L.A. It is a masterpiece in glass and wood overlooking the Pacific Ocean. He died in 1978.

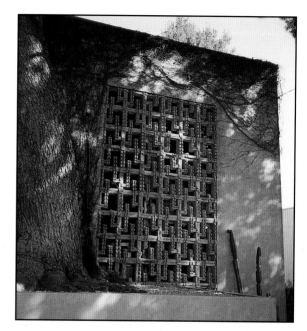

31) Lloyd Wright House, 1928, Lloyd Wright, 858 NORTH DOHENY DRIVE

Notice the "mansionettes" (small scale grand homes) with French Mansard roofs, and town house style front doors and windows. You will also notice the difference between West Hollywood and Beverly Hills in lot sizes and scale of houses.

Turn left on Hammond Street

 Turn right on Sunset Blvd.

32) Right at the top of the street on Sunset Blvd. is another example of Deconstructivist Post-modern architecture. The pink and green building houses offices. The structure of the building is seen on the outside with exposed structural beams in front and the recessed walls clad in square tiles. A colorful palette draws attention to the building.

You are now on the Sunset Strip, known for its wild rock n' roll music clubs of the 1960s, but before that had many elegant nightclubs from the 1940s. Ciro's, Mocambo, and Cafe Trocadero were some of the clubs from the Swing era, which made way for newer clubs like The Roxy, the Key Club, and the Whiskey A Go-Go.

33) Look to your left on the corner of Sunset Blvd. and Clark Street to see the Art Deco-style Whiskey A Go-Go nightclub. Originally built as a Bank of America, it has housed a music club since the early 1960s, where acts like The Doors and Janice Joplin performed and Goldie Hawn was a go-go dancer. It is still an active music venue showcasing new music bands.

32) Pink and Green Office Building, c. 1988, Architectural Collective, 8981 SUNSET BLVD.

33) Bank of America, (now Whiskey A Go-Go), c. 1925, (architect unknown), 8901 Sunset Blvd.

Pass Larrabee Street
Turn right on Holloway Drive

34) Here on your right, next to the Dialog Coffee shop is the site of a series of stores designed by Schindler. They have been altered, however, you can still see a little of the original building that Schindler designed. The angular, boxy forms of the structure and the deeply recessed windows are indications of Schindler's hand.

34) Lingenbrink Stores, 1937, Rudolf M. Schindler, 8758 Holloway Drive

Continue on Holloway Drive
Cross La Cienega Blvd., stay in right lane
Turn left on Santa Monica Blvd.
Right on Kings Road

35) Past Willoughby Avenue, here on your right and just barely visible through the thick bamboo and hedges is the house that Schindler built for himself and his family. Made of tilt-up concrete, with varying levels and a flat roof, it has a communal kitchen and living room and sleeping baskets, or porches, up above. Schindler also designed the outside spaces using them as outdoor rooms. In this house, the architect redefines what a house is both socially and in his use of space and materials because this house was designed for two families to share. Notice the windows, which are mere vertical slits. This is an abstraction and redefinition of what a window is. The use of concrete throughout serves to keep the house cool in the warm southern California climate and the exterior spaces have been recessed to define outdoor rooms.

Schindler came to Los Angeles as an employee of Frank Lloyd Wright's to supervise construction on the Hollyhock House (seen on the HOLLY-WOOD tour). When that was finished he formed his own practice and this was the first house he built. This house is listed on the National Register of Historic Places.

This house is now operated by MAK, an Austrian cultural organization, and is open to the public. A visit inside is well worth it.

35) Schindler House, 1922, Rudolf M. Schindler, 833 NORTH KINGS ROAD

 Turn left on Waring Avenue

36) Here on the left corner of Waring and Sweetzer Avenues are the fantastic Islamic-inspired apartments of the 1920s. Original buildings of this style were built in India, Egypt, and Spain from the 14th century onward. Characteristics of Islamic architecture include domed roofs, pointed arches, and balconies, all of which can be seen here in this early 20th century version.

36) Islamic Revival Apartments, c. 1925, Carl Kay, 801-801 1/2 SWEETZER AVENUE

Turn left on Sweetzer Avenue

37) Next, here on your left is a good example of English Tudor Revival architecture with its half-timber construction (half wood, half masonry), diamond pane windows, and steep wood shingled roof. This complex of apartments was thought have been a real estate investment by Charlie Chaplin, the English-born star of the silent screen. He dabbled in real estate and his name is associated with a number of buildings throughout Los Angeles.

37) "Charlie Chaplin" Apartments, c. 1928, (architect unknown), 819 1/4-825 1/2 SWEETZER AVENUE

 Turn right on Romaine Street

38a & 38b) Here on your left, at the corner of Romaine Street and Harper Avenue are two houses next to each other designed by R.M. Schindler on speculation. These were not commissioned by clients, but built with the intention of selling. This is some of his earliest work in Los Angeles. The other house is on the corner of Romaine Street and La Jolla Street.

38a) House, 1922, Rudolf M. Schindler, 1000 NORTH HARPER AVENUE

39) Here on your left, on the corner of Waring Street and Harper Avenue is a stunning example of the Late Art Deco style known as Streamline Moderne. In the 1930s Art Deco architecture took on a different look. The stock market crash of 1929 led to The Great Depression and the style became much more pared down with no surface ornamentation. Also during this time in history, ocean liner and train travel were beginning to be more popular for the wealthy. This architectural style embraces the machine and reflects the start of the Modern movement. Clean lines and curved corners, including a curved window wall on the first floor and minimalist features such as piping for handrails, all defined this new look. This was the beginning of Modernism.

38b) House, 1922, Rudolf M. Schindler, 8235 ROMAINE STREET

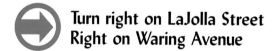

**Turn right on LaJolla Street
Right on Waring Avenue**

39) Duplex Apartments, 1936, William P. Kesling, 754-756 HARPER AVENUE

Map Five

Havenhurst Dr

Fountain Av   45

44

Santa Monica Blvd   Santa Monica Blvd

Crescent Heights Blvd

Orlando Av

Waring Av

La Cienega Blvd

40

43

41   42

Melrose Av

40) Here on your left at the corner of Waring Avenue and La Cienega Blvd. is an elevated brick box. Local architect Craig Ellwood created a pristine and elegant Mid-Century Modern box. A small office building is housed in a steel cage and clad in bricks in a minimalist approach to space enclosure. No surface ornamentation is necessary as the beauty lies in the simplicity of the materials, structure, and form. Housed here are the offices for an accounting firm. Craig Ellwood also designed the Art Center School of Design in Pasadena, along with many other office buildings and private homes in Los Angeles.

Turn left on La Cienega Blvd.

41) On your right, at the corner of Melrose Avenue and La Cienega Blvd. is the black and white marble "striped" building with windows framed in dark pink, built in the mid-1980s. Although the striping of the design actually has its roots in Byzantine architecture, this building is reminiscent of the bold color combinations and patterns of the 1980s.

40) Office Building, 1960, Craig Ellwood, 760 North La Cienega Blvd.

41) "Striped" Building, 1984, A.C. Martin & Associates, 8500 Melrose Avenue

Turn left on Melrose Avenue

42) Across the street, at the corner of Melrose Avenue and La Cienega Blvd., is a tall yellow building with curved green glass that is the addition to the Center for Early Education, designed by Gruen Associates, which is a pre-school and elementary school. Looking more like an office building than a school, there are some hints at playfulness. The dark orange squares at the windows allude to building blocks, and notice the clock tower and the hands on the clock. They were created to look like images of children. Behind the newer building, difficult to see now, is the original school building built in 1989 by local architect Ron Goldman, who used brick, chain link fence, and colorful elements to create an urban school in a densely populated area.

43) Gemini G.E.L. Gallery and Studio, 1979, Frank O. Gehry, 8365 MELROSE AVENUE

43) Coming up on your left, just past Orlando Avenue, is an example of the early work of Frank Gehry. The two-story white box structure at the corner of Melrose Avenue and Kings Road was completed in 1979. The Gemini G.E.L. Studio is the location of an art gallery and artist's print shop. Multiples by Roy Lichtenstein, Robert Rauschenberg, and Richard Serra, among others, have all been produced and exhibited here. In the 1970s, Gehry was interested in creating structures with exposed skeletons, showing their constructive elements. He believed that a building looked better in the process of construction than when it was finished and "the good stuff" was covered over. Here he creates windows specifically to show you the wood studs of the frame construction. He embraces the "unfinished" look. Gehry also embraces the use of industrial materials. Notice the exposed plywood sheets on the side of the building in the parking lot. Once inside, a slightly skewed, wooden staircase takes you to an upstairs gallery where you can see his concept first hand. The gallery is open to the public and a look inside is well worth a stop.

42) The Center for Early Education, c. 1989, Ron Goldman; Addition, 2003, Gruen Associates, 563 NORTH ALFRED STREET

Turn left on Crescent Heights Blvd.

44) Just past the intersection of Crescent Heights Blvd. and Santa Monica Blvd., on your left, is a grey and white Italian Renaissance Revival apartment building. This building was recently transformed. It was formerly painted all one dark color and trees in front were overgrown and hiding the building. The transformation occurred when the trees were trimmed back and the architectural details were painted white. Notice the quoins, painted white to articulate the corners. The window frames and arched doorway are also painted white to contrast with the dark grey background color.

44) Villa Italia Apartments, c. 1930, (architect unknown), 1201 Crescent Heights Blvd.

 ## Get ready to turn left on Fountain Avenue

45) On the southwest corner of Crescent Heights Blvd. and Fountain Avenue is an elegant Chateauesque style apartment building. L-shaped and made of brick, with a steep slate roof and wood casement windows, it is an example of sophisticated apartment living of the 1920s in West Hollywood.

45) La Fontaine, 1928, (architect unknown), 1285-1289 North Crescent Heights Blvd.

 ## Turn left on Fountain Avenue
Quick right on Havenhurst Drive

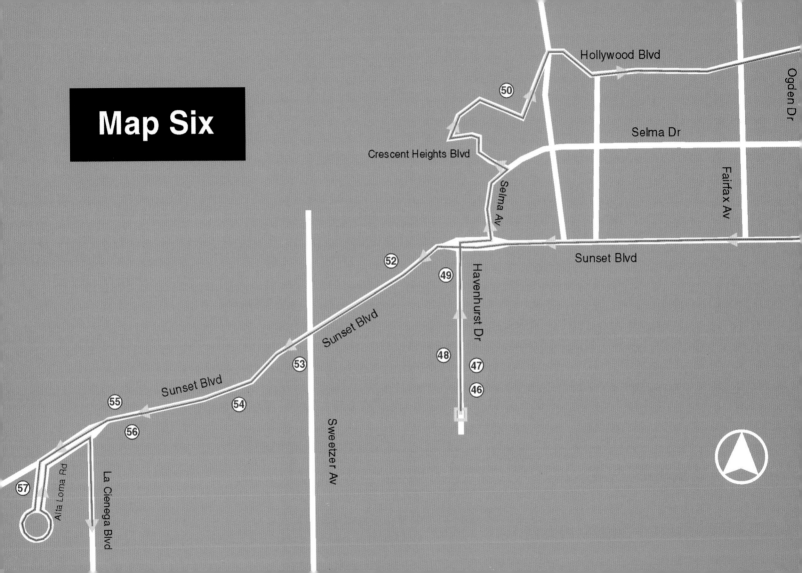

Map Six

Hollywood Blvd

Ogden Dr

50

Selma Dr

Crescent Heights Blvd

Fairfax Av

Selma Av

Sunset Blvd

52

49

Havenhurst Dr

Sunset Blvd

53

48

47

Sweetzer Av

46

55

Sunset Blvd

54

56

Alta Loma Rd

La Cienega Blvd

57

46) On your right is a gem of an apartment building (not converted to condos). The foremost courtyard apartment designers in Los Angeles in the 1920s, husband and wife Arthur and Nina Zwebell designed La Ronda with two distinct interior courtyards. Sixteen apartments, each one different, surround two courtyards with fountains. The Spanish Mediterranean Revival style here is characterized by the deeply recessed windows of various shapes, decorative mosaic tiles, and decorative metal grillwork, balconies, and terra cotta roof. This building is listed on the National Register of Historic Places.

46) La Ronda, 1928, Arthur and Nina Zwebell, 1400 Havenhurst Drive

47) Right next door to La Ronda is a completely different building, designed in the Neo-Georgian style. With green Colonial style shutters and decorative brickwork, it is a very tall, white-painted brick building, and another example of elegant and sophisticated apartment (now condo) living. Former residents include Bette Davis, Eddie Cantor, Sandra Bullock, Tim Burton, and Hugh Grant. This building is listed on the National Register of Historic Places.

47) The Colonial House, 1930, (architect unknown), 1416 Havenhurst Drive

48) Across the street on the left is a Mid-Century Modern apartment building called "The Palmdale House." Composed of geometric angles and a white open frame awning and patio above the parking lot, it appears as though a space ship could land on its deck.

49) On your left is another apartment complex designed by the Zwebell's, so-called "The Andalusia." It is a very romantic courtyard apartment building. It was designed in a hybrid style combining French, Italian, and Spanish Mediterranean architecture. It features a brick motor court, carved wood balconies on the second floor, and decorated garage doors. If you look through the main entrance you can just see the courtyard with central fountain. At one time the building was home to silent screen star Clara Bow and western novelist Louis Lamour. This building is listed on the National Register of Historic Places.

48) Palmdale House, c. 1951, Sanford Kent, 1415-1421 1/2 Havenhurst Drive

49) Andalusia Apartments, 1927, Arthur and Nina Zwebell, 1471-1475 1/2 Havenhurst Drive

Turn right on Sunset Blvd.
Quickly turn left on Selma Avenue
Turn left on Crescent Heights Blvd.
Turn right on Hollywood Blvd.
Continue turning right

50) Here on your left is one of the "textile block" houses designed by Frank Lloyd Wright in the early 1920s. It was originally built for homeopathic physician John Storer. The textile block system of construction was created by Frank Lloyd Wright and consisted of pouring concrete into patterned molds and stringing them all together with steel reinforcing rods. Wright built four of these houses in southern California. (Two are seen on the HOLLYWOOD tour and the other on the PASADENA tour.) The textile block design is carried out on the interior of the house as well. It is 2,967 square feet inside and has three bedrooms and three bathrooms. Since 1984 the house was owned by movie producer Joel Silver and it was badly damaged in the 1994 6.8 Northridge Earthquake. Fortunately, it was fully restored with the help of grandson Eric Lloyd Wright in 1995 and is maintained in good condition by another owner.

50) Storer House, 1923, Frank Lloyd Wright, 8161 HOLLYWOOD BLVD.

Continue down the hill and onto Hollywood Blvd.
Cross Laurel Canyon Blvd. at the traffic light, stay in right lane
Pass Fairfax Avenue
Right on Ogden Drive

51) Past Selma Avenue, here on your left is another home designed by the son of Frank Lloyd Wright. This was built one year before the Storer House just seen. It is much smaller in scale and much more pared down in expression. The rectilinear form, grouping of windows, and lack of surface ornamentation create a Modern house. This house has some elements of the Art Deco Streamline Moderne style, but pre-dates Modernism. Both father and son had overlapping careers, but due to the elder's volatile temperament, they had a number of estrangements during their lifetime. Lloyd Wright was very prolific in Los Angeles.

51) Henry Bollman House, 1922, Lloyd Wright, 1530 NORTH OGDEN DRIVE

➡ Turn right on Sunset Blvd.

52) On your right, as Sunset Blvd. begins to curve, the huge structure on the hill at the start of the Sunset Strip is the Chateau Marmont. Designed in a version of the French Chateauesque style and fashioned after a castle in the Loire Valley, it has been a celebrity haunt since the 1920s. Billy Wilder, Boris Karloff, Howard Hughes, and Marilyn Monroe have all stayed here at one time. More recently, the late photographer Helmut Newton always stayed here when he was in town, as do Stiller and Meara when they're here. Actor John Belushi did himself in here in the early 1980s in one of the bungalows.

53) Thunderbird Inn (now The Standard Hotel), c.1960, (architect unknown), 8300 SUNSET BLVD.

53) Here on your left, at the corner of Sweetzer Avenue, the white three-story Standard Hotel was originally a pretty ordinary motel. Before it was transformed into the Standard by proprietor Andre Balasz in the mid-1990s, however, it was actually a retirement home. Now it is one of the hippest hotels on The Strip due to the resurgence of interest in Mid-Century Modern architecture.

52) Chateau Marmont Hotel, 1929, Arnold Weitzman, Bungalows, 1956, Craig Ellwood, 8221 SUNSET BLVD.

54) Next on your left, the tall greyish building with black glass details is now the very elegant and stylish Argyle Hotel. This is the best example of Art Deco style architecture in all of Los Angeles. With beautiful rounded corners, black glass, and relief sculpture above the entrance depicting zeppelins, airplanes, and pagodas, it was originally designed as an apartment building. This architect designed a number of apartment buildings in L.A., most in the French Chateauesque style, but this was his masterpiece in Los Angeles. This building is listed on the National Register of Historic Places.

55) On your right is an office building with a Japanese restaurant, but it was once an elegant apartment building. On this site in a different building there was a brothel, and at one time recently the building was owned by rock star Rod Stewart. It was restored in the 1980s. This building is listed on the National Register of Historic Places.

54) Sunset Tower (now The Argyle Hotel), 1931, Leland A. Bryant, 8358 Sunset Blvd.

55) Hacienda Arms (now Piazza Del Sol), 1927, (architect unknown), Restoration, c. 1984, (GHI Architects), 8439 Sunset Blvd.

56) Across the street, the large white cube with two enormous wood doors is another hip hotel. This hotel was called the Mondrian Hotel during one of its incarnations due to its color scheme reminiscent of the palette of Dutch artist Piet Mondrian. With squares and rectangles of primary red, blue, and yellow, it looked like a three-dimensional Mondrian painting. When hotelier Ian Schrager acquired the building, it was renovated and remodeled by French architect Philippe Starck, who also designed the Taschen bookstore in Beverly Hills (seen earlier). All of Mondrian's color is gone in favor of a white and beige color scheme.

56) The Mondrian Hotel (renovation), 1996, Philippe Starck, 8440 Sunset Blvd.

 **Turn left on
Alta Loma Road**

57) Here in this tall building with a curved glass front, which was originally the Playboy Building, is the A + D Museum, which features changing exhibitions of architecture and design. Recently opened in this space in 2004, this museum offers free admission and is well worth a visit.

**57) A + D Museum, 2004, (Re-model)
Nadel Architects, 8560 Sunset Blvd.**

 **Turn around on Alta Loma Road
Right on Sunset Blvd.
Right on La Cienega Blvd.**

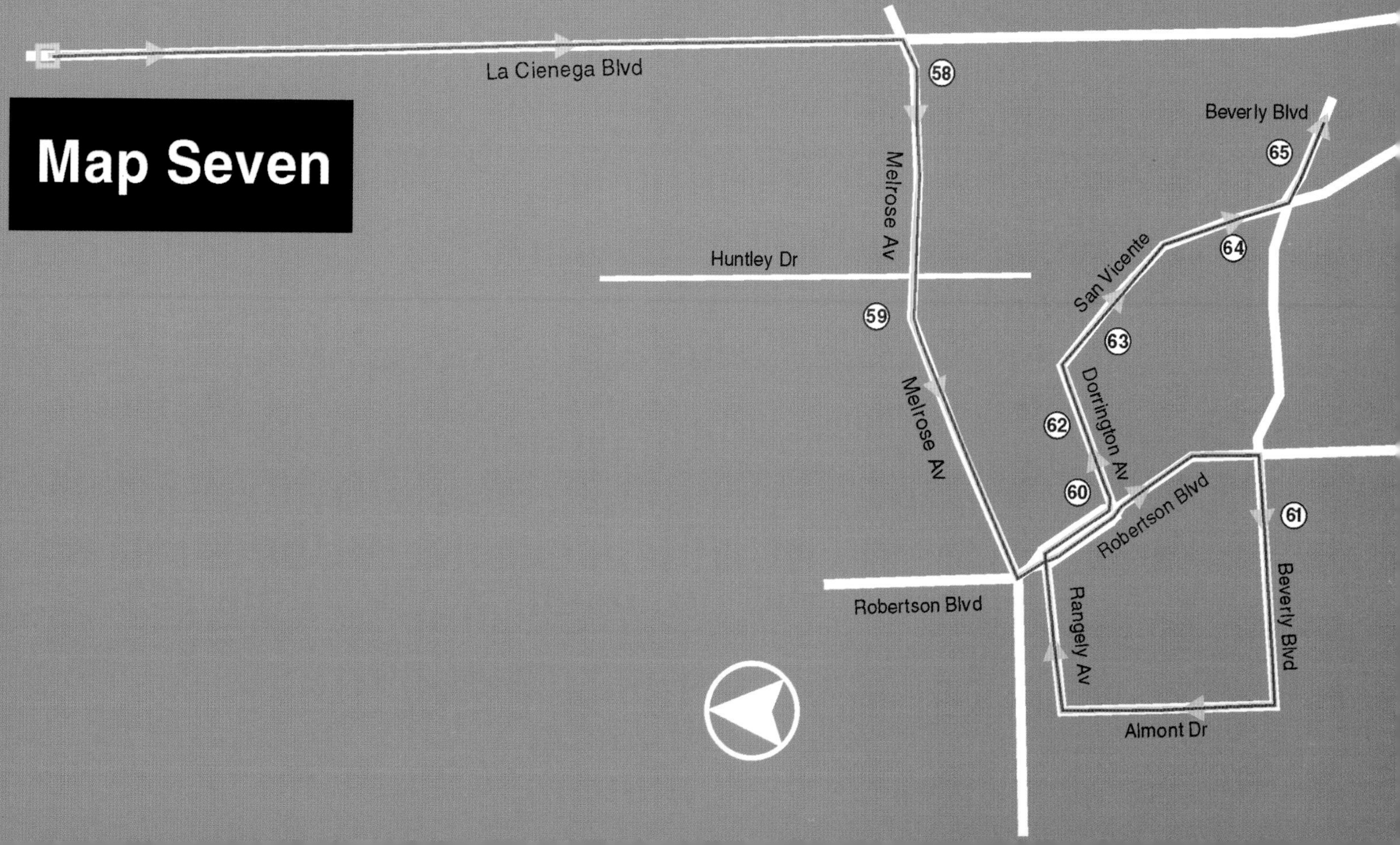

Map Seven

La Cienega Blvd

58

Beverly Blvd

65

Melrose Av

Huntley Dr

San Vicente

64

59

63

Melrose Av

Dorrington Av

62

60

Robertson Blvd

61

Robertson Blvd

Rangely Av

Beverly Blvd

Almont Dr

58) Again you will see the "Striped" Building...

58) "Striped" Building, 1984, A.C. Martin & Associates, 8500 MELROSE AVENUE

 Turn right on Melrose Avenue

59) Just past Huntley Drive, here on your right and impossible to miss, is the massive cobalt blue glass PDC, the location of floors and floors of furniture, fabric, and lighting showrooms for designers and architects. Built in the mid-1970s by Argentine-born architect Cesar Pelli, the side profile of the building is in the shape of the profile of a wave. Affectionately called "The Big Blue Whale," behind it there is a second building clad in green glass panels, built in 1988, and third building is currently in the planning stages. Pelli also designed the World Financial Center and the Winter Garden in New York City.

59) Pacific Design Center, 1975, Cesar Pelli (Gruen Associates), 8687 Melrose Avenue

This area is called "Avenues of Art and Design" and there are many showrooms at street level for interior designers and architects as well as many contemporary art galleries

 Turn left on Robertson Blvd.

60) Turtle Sculpture at The Remba Gallery, 1999, Jonathan Borofsky, 462 ROBERTSON BLVD.

60) On your left, past Rangely Avenue, are the Koplin Del Rio and Remba Galleries. Above the entrance to the Remba Gallery is a kinetic sculpture by artist Jonathan Borofsky. It is an organized grouping of seventy-two cast copper turtles whose heads bob in and out in a slow, methodical way. The grand scale sculpture reads as one as you pass by it, and then by looking closer you can see the individual turtles, all working as one. The artist uses the turtle, an ancient being, to symbolize the passage of time, and this sculpture actually functions as a timepiece. The hour is indicated by the number of the column in which the turtle heads are bobbing. The Remba Gallery specializes in artist's prints and has created a technique for printmaking called Mixografia.

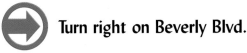 **Turn right on Beverly Blvd.**

61) On the south side of Beverly Blvd, just west of Robertson Blvd., is the showroom originally designed by Charles Eames, well-known for his furniture designs, for the retailer of his furniture. The front wall is a sheet of glass with black mullions. The walls are made of brick. This is a simple box to showcase beautiful furniture.

61) Herman Miller Showroom (now SEE), 1949, Charles Eames, 8806 Beverly Blvd.

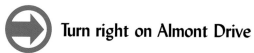 **Turn right on Almont Drive**

Notice the small scale "mansionette" houses in this neighborhood.

Right on Rangely Avenue
Right on Robertson Blvd.
Left on Dorrington Avenue

62) Here on your left is one of the largest houses on this street. Designed by architect Gilberto for himself and his family, he outgrew it and moved on when another child was born in 2003. Trying to get the most square footage out of the lot, the house covers nearly all of it and is as tall as possible. Exposed bow trusses in the living room, and walls of glass in front allow light to come in while the side walls are closed for privacy. There is even a small swimming pool in back.

62) House, 2001, Gilberto, 8735 Dorrington Avenue

Turn right on San Vicente Blvd.

63) Here on your right, at the corner of Ashcroft Avenue, the two-story structure was originally designed for designer Michael Morrison, who lived in the upper level and had his showroom on the ground level. A simple composition of concrete and glass, it was renovated and is now a private home for art dealers who also use it as a showcase for art, by appointment only.

63) Morrison House, c. 1984, Kirk Florence, 417 North San Vicente Blvd.

64) Coming up on your right, just before Beverly Blvd., is a favorite work of architecture. The hot dog stand called "Tail-O-The-Pup" has been serving hot dogs for years. This is an example of Programmatic, or Roadside architecture, where the building takes on the shape of the thing it's trying to sell, thereby grabbing your attention as you drive by.

64) Tail-O-The-Pup, 1946, Milton J. Black, 343 NORTH SAN VICENTE BLVD.

65) Across the street on the corner of San Vicente Blvd. and Beverly Blvd. is the fairly new Imaging Center, part of the complex of medical buildings that comprise Cedars-Sinai Medical Center across the street. It is clad in slate stone and incorporates the bus stop seating area right into the design by continuing the stone down to the street. Green glass is also used at the corner.

65) Imaging Center, c. 1999, Rockland, Baron & Balboa, 310 NORTH SAN VICENTE BLVD.

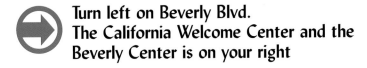

**Turn left on Beverly Blvd.
The California Welcome Center and the
Beverly Center is on your right**

SELECTED BIBLIOGRAPHY

Gebhard, David, and Robert Winter. *Los Angeles: An Architectural Guide*. Layton, Utah: Gibbs Smith Publisher, 1994.

Gierach, Ryan. *Images of America: West Hollywood*. Charleston, South Carolina: Arcadia Publishing, 2003.

Gleye, Paul. *The Architecture of Los Angeles*. Los Angeles: Rosebud Books-The Knapp Press, 1981.

Heimann, Jim. *California Crazy & Beyond Roadside: Vernacular Architecture*. San Francisco: Chronicle Books, 2001.

Herr, Jeffrey (edited by). *Landmark L.A.: Historic-Cultural Monuments of Los Angeles*. City of Los Angeles Cultural Affairs Department, Santa Monica, California: Angel City Press, 2002.

Kaplan, Sam Hall. *L.A. Lost and Found: An Architectural History of Los Angeles*. New York: Crown Publishers, 1987.

McGrew, Patrick and Robert Julian. *Landmarks of Los Angeles*. New York: Harry N. Abrams Publishers, 1994.

Index of Architects